THE UNOFFICIAL AEROGARDEN BIBLE

Everything You Need to Know to Grow an Edible Indoor Garden Without Dirt, Bugs or a Green Thumb!

By Julia Clarkson

HHF Press

San Francisco

COPYRIGHT © 2020 Healthy Happy Foodie Press (HHF Press)

First published 2020

All rights reserved. No part of this book may be reproduced in any form or by any electronic or mechanical means, including information storage and retrieval systems, without permission in writing from the publisher, except by reviewers, who may quote brief passages in a review.

Editor: HHF Press

Art Direction: HHF Press

Illustrations: HHF Press

All photographs in this book © HHF Press, © Shutterstock.com or © Depositphotos.com

Published in the United States of America by HHF Press

268 Bush St, #3042

San Francisco, CA 94104 USA

www.HHFPress.com

Disclaimer:

Although the publisher and authors of this book are practically obsessed with modern cooking techniques, neither the publisher nor the authors represent or are affiliated with any of the brands mentioned in this text.

All content herein represents the authors' own experiences and opinions, and do not represent medical or health advice. The responsibility for the consequences of your actions, including your use or misuse of any suggestion or procedure described in this book lies not with the authors, publisher or distributors of this book. We recommend using common sense and consulting with a licensed health professional before changing your diet or exercise. The authors or the publisher do not assume any liability for the use of or inability to use any or all of the information contained in this book, nor do the authors or publisher accept responsibility for any type of loss or damage that may be experienced by the user as the result of activities occurring from the use of any information in this book. Use the information responsibly and at your own risk.

The authors and publisher reserve the right to make changes he or she deems required to future versions of the publication to maintain accuracy.

CONTENTS

- 1   WHAT IS AN AEROGARDEN?
- 5   ABOUT COUNTERTOP GARDENING
- 9   HOW DOES THE AEROGARDEN WORK?
- 13   WHAT CAN YOU GROW IN AN AEROGARDEN?
- 23   HOW TO USE YOUR AEROGARDEN
- 33   PRO TIPS
- 37   RECIPES
  - 38   Bruschetta al Pomodoro
  - 39   Fresh Green Salad
  - 40   Homemade Mint Ice Cream
  - 41   Instant Pot Thai Green Curry
  - 42   Chimichurri de Buenos Aires
  - 43   Chermoula
  - 44   Classic Avocado Toast with Cherry Tomatoes
  - 45   Shishito Poppers
  - 46   Pimientos Rellenos
  - 47   Basil Pesto
  - 48   Classic Meatballs
  - 49   Spaghetti with Fresh Tomato and Basil
  - 50   Honeyed Carrots
  - 51   Arugula Salad with Citrus
  - 52   Caesar Salad with Grilled Romaine
  - 53   Cilantro and Tomato Chicken
  - 54   Salsa Fresca
  - 55   Creamy Mashed Potatoes
  - 56   Asian-Style Salad
  - 57   Zucchini Soup with Basil
  - 58   Turkey Stuffing
  - 59   Frittata with Tomatoes
  - 60   Hummus with Jalapeños
  - 61   Asian-Style Grilled Chicken Wraps
  - 62   Red Wine Vinaigrette
  - 63   Mint Mojito
  - 64   Zoodles with Tomatoes
  - 65   Kale Caesar salad
  - 66   Risotto with Fresh Herbs
  - 67   Ranch dressing

CHAPTER 1

WHAT IS AN AEROGARDEN?

Quite simply, the Aerogarden® is a revolutionary way to garden, in the comfort of your own home, all year round. By using a system of high-powered LED lights, the Aerogarden creates enough light to grow a wide array of different plants right in your kitchen (or whichever room you choose).

But the Aerogarden isn't just for seasoned gardeners with bright green thumbs. It's is also perfect for those of you who have had trouble gardening in the past. That's because the Aerogarden allows you to get started by using seed pods designed specifically for the Aerogarden. No matter which model you choose, the Aerogarden will bring healthy fun to the whole family.

Let's talk a bit about the different models and which one is right for you.

THE AEROGARDEN MODELS

The Sprout

This is the newest addition to the Aerogarden family. The Sprout is also the smallest Aerogarden and is perfect for those who have very limited space or only want to grow a few plants at a time. This model allows you to grow up to three seed pods at one time. The unit's grow hood comes equipped with sixty individual LED lights which offer an even distribution of light over the growing surface. This means that you won't have to worry about adjusting the lighting hood in order to ensure even growing.

Because the lights in all of the Aerogarden models are LED, you don't need to worry about the lights causing unwanted extra heat in your home. That's the first great thing about LED lights. The second benefit of using LEDs is that they draw very little power, so you don't have to worry about getting a huge electricity bill.

In addition to these great features, the Sprout also features an extendable lighting arm which allows you to increase the height of the lights as your plants start to grow.

The bottom line is that, if you are a beginner and want to start growing your own vegetables, or if you have very limited space, the Sprout may be the perfect model for you. It is the simplest and easiest of the Aerogardens to use and sets up in minutes.

The Harvest Series

This is the most popular family of Aerogardens because they allow you to grow up to six plants at one time, but they are also very compact and easy to use. The Harvest Series is comprised of six different models which are separated into two categories: standard and elite. The standard models feature simpler controls and come in three different configurations.

The standard Harvest is 10.5 inches wide and 7.5 inches deep, making it a good fit for most kitchen counters. If, however, you have especially shallow counters, or you just want to save some space, you can choose the Harvest Slim model which is wider at 15 inches but narrower at only 5 inches.

Finally, there is the Harvest 360, which features the same grow area as the other two models but in a round configuration.

The Elite models in the Harvest series feature real stainless-steel construction as well as digital displays and lighted buttons to make using the control even easier. They also feature a smaller footprint that the standard series without sacrificing grow area or water capacity.

The Bounty Series

For those looking for more space and versatility, the Bounty Series allows you to grow up to nine plants at one time and features forty watts of full spectrum LED light. This allows you to grow plants up to five times faster than plants grown in soil. The Bounty Series is available in a range of different finishes, but all of the models in this series feature the same grow space and lighting.

The Farm Family Series

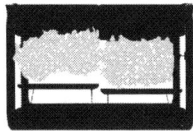

Finally, for those looking for a serious indoor gardening experience there is the Farm Family Series which allows you to grow either twelve or twenty-four pods at the same time. This series requires a considerable amount of space, but it will yield enough fresh vegetables and herbs that you can probably avoid trips to the supermarket altogether.

The Farm 12 allows you to grow twelve pods at the same time and features sixty watts of growing power. Keep in mind that the Farm Family Series models are not meant to be placed on a countertop because they are simply too large. These models are appropriate when you have adequate floorspace to accommodate their large footprints.

If you are looking to keep your footprint small but instead grow vertically, the Farm 12XL has the same footprint as the Farm 12 but is twice as tall.

Finally, the Farm 24 Series is for indoor gardeners looking for ultimate space and flexibility. The Farm 24 series features sixty watts of full spectrum LED power, but it comes split into two LED panels. This means you can have the panels at different heights to customize your growing experience even more. The Farm 24 Series features both a standard and XL height model allowing you to grow as high as you need. As an added bonus, the Farm Family Series models come with touch screens and Amazon Alexa connectivity for ultimate ease of use.

No matter what your situation, there is sure to be an Aerogarden that fits your needs and your space. As we've previously mentioned, the Aerogarden is a little different from conventional gardening. Apart from the Aerogarden being used indoors, it differs from conventional gardening because it uses hydroponic technology instead of conventional soil growing. So, let's discuss how hydroponic gardening works.

CHAPTER 2

ABOUT COUNTERTOP GARDENING

HOW DOES COUNTERTOP GARDENING WORK?

As you probably know, there are two main components to how plants grow. They need a light source to allow them to perform photosynthesis, and they need water and nutrients delivered to their roots.

Traditionally, plants grow in soil and this provides the water and nutrients they need. The sun provides the other part of the equation by showering the plant with light that allows the plant to turn that nutrition into energy.

Hydroponic gardening, on the other hand, cuts out one crucial component of the process: the soil. Soil itself isn't essential for plant growth as long as the plants can still get the water and nutrients they need.

THE BENEFITS OF HYDROPONIC GARDENING

So why is hydroponic gardening such a great option? Well, the whole idea of hydroponic growing is control. Instead of your plants being at the mercy of their outdoor environment, you can control the nutrition, water quality, and light. As you may know, some soil is simply more nutritious than other types of soil. While you can add nutrients to soil to make it more fertile, this becomes a complicated process that you can't really test without using sophisticated equipment.

Hydroponic gardening, on the other hand, allows you full control of your plant's environment. You can control exactly how pure the water is, and you can decide exactly which nutrients to add and in what amounts. This also means that you can achieve greater consistency over the course of the whole year.

Most people live in climates that change drastically throughout the year. For many people, this means that growing plants outdoors in the winter is simply impossible. The soil is frozen, the air temperature is too cold, and there isn't enough light. With hydroponic gardening, none of these factors are a concern. You can grow plants just as well in the winter as in the summer because all of these factors are well within your control.

Hydroponic gardening works by feeding your plants a constant supply of fresh, nutrient rich water, while also providing high-powered artificial light by way of an energy-efficient LED panel. In recent years, LED technology has exploded, allowing for the lights to be made more cheaply and in greater numbers. LEDs are also perfect because they don't require a lot of energy to create bright, nourishing lights. That means your electricity bill probably won't be affected very much.

NOURISHING YOUR PLANTS

Depending on what you are growing, you may want to change the pH balance of your water or add different nutrients that support your plants. Typically, plants need a steady diet of magnesium, phosphorus, and calcium in order to grow well. By adding these nutrients yourself, you can always be sure that your plants are getting exactly what they need. When you grow in soil—even when using fertilizer—you can never really be sure of exactly what is being absorbed into the soil and ultimately into your plants. Hydroponic gardening, on the other hand, allows for greater precision and control.

So, what does all this mean in terms of results? Part of the reason hydroponic gardening has become so popular with professional farms as well as amateur gardeners is because you can expect much higher plant yields than with

traditional farming methods. This is because the roots of your plants will have an easier job than if they were growing in the soil.

With regular gardening, the plants task their roots with finding nutrients and water. Depending on how difficult this is for the roots, they may have to devote a lot of energy to forming a complex root system in order to find what they need in order to thrive. Because the plants are using this energy to form an extensive root system, they don't have as much energy left over to grow upward and produce vegetables.

When you grow hydroponically, the plant doesn't need to expend this energy in order to find nutrients and water. The plants have everything they need, brought straight to their roots. Because of this, the plants are able to channel all of their energy into upward growth. Not only will you achieve higher yields and larger plants, but you will, most likely, notice that your plants start to sprout earlier than if they were planted in soil. This happens because the seeds have more direct contact with the nutrient rich water which speeds up the germination process.

As you can see, there are many benefits to countertop gardening. It's cleaner, it's faster, and you will end up with bigger plants with higher yields. When you consider all of these benefits, it's no wonder that so many commercial farmers have converted to hydroponic systems for many of their crops.

Oh, and there's one more benefit that shouldn't be overlooked: Safety. Because many plants sprout directly from the soil with no stem or branches, the parts that you eat can be in direct contact with fertilizer. In some cases, this fertilizer can cause illnesses like e. coli poisoning because the e. coli bacteria are found in fertilized soil.

When you grow hydroponically, you don't ever have to worry about this because your plants will be grown in seeds pods that do not use harmful fertilizers.

CHAPTER 3

HOW DOES THE AEROGARDEN WORK?

We've already discussed the science of hydroponic growing, so now let's take some time to discuss exactly how your Aerogarden works.

BASIC PRINCIPLES: BASE AND LIGHTS

Every model of Aerogarden works based on the same basic principles. The base of the unit is where you will place the seed pods and the water. Above the growing area is a panel containing LED lights, which will provide all of the light your growing plants need in order to thrive.

So, why are LEDs the best choice for countertop gardening. In short, it's because they are very powerful and consume very little electricity. They also have the benefit of producing hardly any heat at all. This factor has been a game changer for indoor gardeners because in the past, the lights that provided enough light to grow plants also produced a lot of heat. This meant the only way to successfully grow plants indoor was to have a complicated ventilation system. Luckily, the advances in LED technology has changed everything. Your Aerogarden will get quite bright, but it shouldn't change the temperature of the room it's in.

The other big advantage of LED lighting is that you won't have to worry about the impact on your power bill. Traditionally, very bright lights consume a lot of energy, and this can get expensive whey you are running the lights for many hours at a time. Because LEDs are so energy efficient, you most likely won't have to spend any extra money on electricity.

WHAT'S INCLUDED?

First, let's make sure you understand everything that is included with your Aerogarden. The garden itself comes preassembled so you don't have to worry about attaching the light panel to the base. There is also a power adapter included, and it's important that you only use this power adapter because it is specifically designed for the Aerogarden. Using other adapters can damage the garden permanently.

You should also have six seed pods and six grow domes if you are using the Aerogarden Harvest Series. Other models will have more or fewer seed pods and grow domes. You will also find a bottle of plant food and instructions for how much food to use are on the bottle.

In order to get started, all you have to do in plug the power adapter into the unit and plug into an outlet. Find the "Fill to Here" line on the base and add water to the line. Then add the recommended amount of plant food to the water.

On the grow deck, you will see six holes for the seed pods. All you need to do is insert the pods into the holes and then loosely cover the pods with the grow domes.

THE TIMER

Now, let's discuss how the timer works. Since you're not a full-time gardener, it can be tricky to remember to turn the lights on and off, so the Aerogarden has made this part a lot easier. When you first turn on your Aerogarden, the LED light panel will turn on.

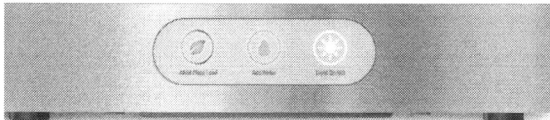

As soon as the lights turn on, the timer has started. You don't need to do anything else. The lights will then stay on for fifteen hours and then automatically turn off. But what if you need to change the light cycle for some reason? For example, say you have the lights set to come on at 9:00 am. If this is the case, the lights will stay on until 12 midnight. But what if you don't want the lights to be on that late. At 6:00 am simply press and hold the Light on/off button for three seconds. The lights will turn on and then off. This will confirm that the light cycle timing has been changed. The lights will now turn on at 6:00 am and turn off at 9:00 pm.

WATER

Obviously, a big part of growing plants is making sure they have the right amount of water. The Aerogarden makes this as easy as it can be. When you first set up your Aerogarden, you will fill the base with water up to the "Fill to Here" line. In order to add more water, all you need to do it remove the water cover and pour in more water. To help you keep track of exactly when to add more water, the Aerogarden has a built-in sensor which will let you know to add more water by flashing the red "Add Water" light on the front of the unit. While the Aerogarden will remind you when it's time to add more water, you don't need to wait for the "Add Water" light to come on. You can always add more water so that the level is at the "Fill to Here" line.

PLANT FOOD

Finally, you will want to make sure you are adding plant food to the water regularly. When plants are grown in soil, they get most of their nutrients right from the soil itself, but when you grow hydroponically, you need to make sure to add plant food to the water because this is the only way your plants will get the nutrition they need.

Luckily, you won't have to add plant food to the Aerogarden very often. The Aerogarden has a built-in timer to remind you to add plant food every two weeks. All you have to do to get started is add plant food to the water when you first set up the garden. Two weeks later, the "Add Plant Food" light will come on, and you can add the recommended amount of plant food to the water. Make sure to add water when you add food so that the water level comes back to the "Fill to Here" line.

FINAL THOUGHTS

If you start a new garden and want to reset the plant food timer, all you have to do is press the plant food timer button for five seconds. The button will flash, and this means that the timer has been reset. You can add your new seed pods to the unit, and make sure the water level is correct.

The water is kept in constant circulation and this will help to make sure the nutrients are evenly distributed around the plant's roots. Because the Aerogarden plant food is specifically formulated to work with the Aerogarden, you don't need to worry about adding any other nutrients to the water. The unique design of the Aerogarden is meant to take all of the guesswork out of the growing process so that you can sit back and enjoy watching your plants grow.

CHAPTER 4

WHAT CAN YOU GROW IN AN AEROGARDEN?

The Aerogarden is meant to be used with the specially designed seed pods that come with your garden. You can also order new and different seed pods depending on what you feel like growing. When you order your Aerogarden, you will be given a choice about which seed pod pack you would like included with the unit. The Harvest Series allows you to plant up to six seeds pods at a time, and you can choose between the following pod packs: Gourmet herbs, heirloom garden salad, cascading petunias, or cherry tomatoes.

(If you visit the Aerogarden website, you can find all of the available seed pods, and you will see that there are dozens of different pods to choose from that allow you to grow a vast array of vegetables, herbs, and flowering plants.)

So, how do the pods work, exactly?

The pods are prepackaged with a special material that holds the seeds in place, as well as specially formulated plant food, which will help the seeds to start germinating almost immediately. In order to get your plants to start germinating as fast as possible, removable grow domes are included, and they fit right over the top of the pod. These domes allow in just enough light, and they keep the conditions in the pod just right to help the seeds germinate.

Typically, you should start to see your seeds germinate in about seven to fourteen days. Because of ambient temperature, the seeds may sprout a little earlier or later. Most herb pods will be ready to harvest in about four to six weeks, and they will continue to keep producing herbs for another six months.

Vegetable seed pods will take a little longer to harvest, but Aerogarden has specially formulated their seeds to produce higher yields than other seed varieties. This way, you can expect to have fresh tomatoes and peppers all year round.

> You might be wondering if you can grow seeds in the Aerogarden without the use of the seed pods. The answer is, yes, but you will need to find certain pieces of equipment in order to do so. We'll talk about that a little later in the book.

GROWING TIMES & YIELDS

Now, let's talk about how long it will take to grow certain items in your Aerogarden. Keep in mind that larger Aerogarden models with larger, higher powered light panels will achieve higher yields and faster results than smaller models. For these estimates, we're going to focus on growing time and yields for the Aerogarden Harvest Series.

WHAT CAN YOU GROW IN YOUR AEROGARDEN?

So, what kinds of vegetables and herbs should you consider growing in your Aerogarden? Again, this will depend somewhat on which Aerogarden model you are using. The larger models will accommodate plants that need to grow higher, while the smaller models are better suited for smaller plants. The Aerogarden Harvest Series is perfect for growing a variety of smaller plants that can be used in a variety of ways. The size of the unit allows you to grow almost any type of herb that you can think of, but just because it's on the smaller side doesn't mean that you can't also grow quite a few different veggies and berries.

Growing Times & Yields

Herbs
Germination 3 to 14 days
Fully grown 35 to 40 days

Vegetables like Tomatoes and Peppers
Germination 7 to 14 days
Fully grown 12 to 14 weeks

Salad Greens
Germination 7 to 14 days
Fully grown 28 to 35 days

Flowers
Germination 7 to 14 days
Fully grown 30 to 40 days

Berries
Germination 5 to 14 days
Fully grown 6 to 10 weeks

Small Vegetables

Cherry tomatoes and small peppers are perfect for smaller Aerogardens and a number of different seed pods are available depending on

which varieties you prefer. If you want to grow sweet peppers, there is a pod for that, but you also have the option of growing some seriously spicy peppers as well. Because the Aerogarden allows you to grow vegetable year-round, you can always count on having fresh veggies for salads or cooking at any time.

Lettuce

Lettuces are also perfect for the Aerogarden,

partly because the Aerogarden will allow you to achieve higher yields than with traditional gardening.

Fresh Flowers

If you find that you miss having fresh flowers during the winter months, you can easily solve this problem by using one of the many seed pods pre-loaded with different varieties of colorful flowers.

When considering what kind of flowers to grow, keep in mind the size of your Aerogarden model because flowers that grow tall will have trouble getting enough light once they reach a certain size. Regardless of what you choose to grow, keep in mind that the LED light panel needs to be located above the tops of your plants, ideally with an inch or two of space between the tops of the plants and the lights.

Medicinal Herbs

One of the other things that many Aerogarden users love is the ability to grow a fresh supply of medicinal herbs. These herbs are often found in dried forms in health food stores, but it is generally recognized by herbal specialists

that fresh herbs provide superior benefits over dried herbs. Having a constant supply of these fresh herbs is an enormous benefit.

Fresh Produce During Winter

During the winter months, fresh produce can be difficult to find depending on where you live. Many people live in places where fresh produce

needs to travel all the way across the country, and in some cases, from other countries. The reality is that the longer fresh produce takes to reach its destination, the less fresh it will be once it arrives.

While the Aerogarden won't be able to provide all of the fresh produce you need, it will allow you to always have a fresh supply of certain fruits and vegetables. Adding additional Aerogardens or upgrading to a larger model will give you even more flexibility and variety.

> Many Aerogarden users are fond of using several Aerogardens at the same time to rotate their harvest. This method will allow you to always have produce to harvest. While one garden is germinating, another can be growing to full size, while a third garden is ready for harvest. By keeping your gardens staggered, you can always have fresh produce on hand.

WHAT CAN YOU NOT GROW IN AN AEROGARDEN?

So, we've discussed what you can grow in the Aerogarden, but we should also discuss what you can't grow in the Aerogarden. Keep in mind that each model of Aerogarden has its own capabilities. A smaller model won't be able to grow as many plants, and it won't allow those plants to grow as large as they would get in one of the larger models.

For most people, the Aerogarden will not grow enough produce to sustain your diet. Because of the size of even the largest Aerogarden, you won't be able to grow enough to provide all of the produce you need.

Additionally, you won't be able to grow very large plants or flowers like sunflowers because they are simply too tall for even the largest Aerogarden. It is also not recommended that you grow plants that, by their nature, require a large, complex root system. As we've already discussed, the Aerogarden allows you to grow plants without them having to develop a large root system, but some plants just prefer to grow that way. In order to keep the plants from damaging the other plants in your Aerogarden, it's best to avoid these types of plants.

You will also not be able to grow flowers that have a bulb root. These types of flowers will not fit comfortably within the size constraints of the Aerogarden pod system.

WHO USES AN AEROGARDEN?

The City Dweller

The Aerogarden is a great tool for anyone who wants to garden, but it's particularly good for certain people because of their particular circumstances. Many city-dwellers would love to spend time gardening and have the benefits of fresh herbs, vegetables, and flowers, but the problem with living in many cities is that you don't have any outdoor space of your own for gardening. The Aerogarden completely solves this problem because it doesn't require any outdoor space at all. It doesn't even require natural sunlight!

Regardless of how big a space you have, there is an Aerogarden that can work for you. If your goal is just a small, countertop herb garden, the three-pod Sprout model is probably perfect for you. If you'd like to expand a bit and start growing fruits and vegetables, you can move up to the Harvest Series. And if you want to devote a large part of your indoor space to gardening, the Family Farm Series gives you maximum growing space and versatility.

Because growing with the Aerogarden is so easy and clean, you won't have to worry about spilled water or soil in your living space, and the quite water circulator won't cause too much noise.

The "Black Thumb"

Many people have had bad experiences with gardening in the past. These people often refer to themselves as having a "black thumb." Bad experiences with garden can be due to a number of different factors. Some people simply don't have the time to consistently keep their garden watered or fed. Other people have trouble with knowing how to space their plants. Still other have bad results through no fault of their own; they simply live in a place that does not have good quality soil or enough moisture in the air.

Regardless of the problems you've had in the past, the Aerogarden removes many of the problematic variables from gardening. If you find that you often forget to water or feed your plants, the Aerogarden solves this by doing all of the watering and feeding for you. If you forget that it's time to add more water to the basin, it will remind you.

If you've had trouble knowing how to position your plants and find that they don't grow properly as a result, you will be happy to find that the Aerogarden has pre-made holes that allow you to perfectly space your plants. And if your problem stems from the fact that the soil in your area is poor quality, the Aerogarden doesn't use soil at all. As long as you have

access to regular tap water, you can grow quality produce in your Aerogarden.

Family Fun

The other great thing about the Aerogarden is that it's great for the whole family. Gardening is a rewarding activity that teaches kids not only about healthy eating, but about science in general. Unfortunately, we as a society, have moved away from growing our own food. We tend to think that food comes from the supermarket instead of from farms, and because of this, we miss out on one of the most amazing parts of life!

The Aerogarden is a fun way to teach kids about the lifecycle of plants. They will get to see, close up, exactly how a plant goes from a seed to a sprout to a full-grown plant. This will give them a better understanding about how plants work, and about where food comes from. It's also an excellent way to teach children about the value of fresh produce. For the majority of us who simply grab fruits and vegetables at the grocery store, we don't really think about where our food comes from. Was it grown organically at a local farm, or has it traveled thousands of miles before it gets to us. As we've said previously, produce loses nutrition the longer it travels, but that's not the only problem with food miles.

The Environmentalist

More and more of us are becoming concerned about the grave danger of climate change, one of the biggest contributing factors of which is shipping. The farther our food travels, the more carbon emissions are released into the atmosphere. Climate scientists have been stressing the fact that in order to reduce carbon emissions we need to cut down on the distance that our food travels.

The Aerogarden is a perfect way to teach children about the value of locally grown food in a nutritional sense and in a global sense. If we are going to tackle our climate problems, we're going to need to change the mindset of the next generation when it comes to how we make food, and how we consume food.

And this brings us to another extremely important point: In addition to a climate crisis, we are facing an obesity crisis. This is happening primarily because we are substituting unhealthy processed foods for the healthier natural foods people used to eat. If you're a parent, you know that it can be difficult to get kids to eat their vegetables.

One of the great ways to encourage kids to get more veggies into their diet is to allow them to be a part of the process. When vegetables come home from the supermarket, kids don't have any sort of connection with it. It's just a food they would rather not eat. But when kids get to see the whole process from beginning to end, they develop a connection with the vegetables they are growing, and they become more inclined to want to eat them.

But avoiding commercial produces isn't just for kids. We would all like to be eating healthier produce and produce that we can rely on. While most commercial farming is safe these days, we are all aware that much of our food is grown with powerful chemical fertilizers and other chemicals to fight weeds.

Because the label of "organic" is somewhat flexible, even those foods can have added pesticides or other chemicals. As a result, growing your own produces is always a safer alternative to commercial produce. And because you will be able to pick it fresh, it will always taste better than produce from the supermarket.

THE HISTORY OF HYDROPONIC GARDENING

Believe it or not, the history of hydroponics goes all the way back to 1627. The first mention of growing plants in water rather than soil was found in a passage by Francis Bacon in his book, 'A Natural History.' Scientists at the time were investigating why plants seemed to grow better in regular water than distilled water (water which has had its minerals removed). It took several hundred years before scientists identified the nine essential elements for plant growth, and this led to a greater understanding of how to grow plants in soil as well as water. This also helped scientists in the 1900s understand why certain soil conditions were either good or bad for plant growth.

Over the next several decades, there was considerably disagreement between botanists over the benefits of hydroponic farming with some scientist arguing that using the hydroponic method wasn't actually any better than growing in soil. However, by the 1960s it had become generally accepted that there were numerous advantages to the hydroponic method, chief among them the fact that it would allow people to grow food in climates that did not support the cultivation of certain plants.

Once advancements like more efficient lighting became available, it became apparent that hydroponic farming was going to result in a revolution of clean, healthy food that could be produced with far less than land traditional farming.

Today, hydroponic farming has become common and is one of the reasons why we can rely on having certain seasonal fruits and vegetables all year round. It is also helping developing communities find new and innovative ways of offering their populations better nutrition and more food.

CHAPTER 5

HOW TO USE YOUR AEROGARDEN

WHAT YOU WILL NEED TO GET STARTED

Luckily, everything you need to get started comes with your Aerogarden (except for the water, of course). In order to assemble the growing surface, place the base of the unit on a level surface. Because it will be filled with water you will want to make sure it is level. Place the grow deck onto the base of the unit. It should fit easily. If you are using a model from the Harvest Series, you will notice that the grow deck has six holes in it. This is where the seed pods will be placed. There is an opening on one side of the grow deck for adding water and plant food. Once you have assembled the grow deck, plug the unit in and turn it on.

You can add water and plant food at this point, and make sure the water does not go over the "Fill to Here" line. The plant food bottle will tell you how much food to add to the water. You can turn on the lights by pushing the "Light" button. This button allows you to turn the lights on and off whenever you would like, and it will not interfere with the lighting timer. If you turn the lights on, they will still turn off when the timer goes off. In order to set the timer to your desired time, simply hold down the light button for three seconds. The lights will flash, and the timer is now set. The lights will stay on for fifteen hours and then automatically turn off.

LEARNING THE CONTROLS

The great thing about all of the Aerogarden models is they feature controls you can learn in seconds. That's because the Aerogardens are designed to be easy to use and completely foolproof.

1. The "Light" button:

On the front of the unit, you will find the "light" button that is used to turn the lights on and off and to set the light timer. All you have to do is hold the button down for three seconds and the lights will flash, indicating that the timer has been set. If you decide you want to change the timer, all you have to do is hold down the light button again for three seconds and the lights will now be adjusted. The light cycle is fifteen hours long, meaning the lights will be on for fifteen hours and off for nine hours.

Because the Aerogarden gives off a lot of light, most gardeners prefer to time their Aerogarden with their own sleep schedule, with the Aerogarden being off when they are sleeping.

2. "Add water" light

The add water light will come on whenever the water level in the tank goes under half-full. You can also keep track of the water level by looking at the
"Fill to here" line.

Luckily, that's all there is to using your Aerogarden!

3. "Add food" light

You will also notice on the front of the panel that there is an "add food" light and an "add water light." The add food light will come on about every two weeks to remind you to add a bit more food to the water tank.

THE LIGHTING PANEL

If you're wondering why the lights stay on for fifteen hours, it's because this has been determined to be the optimal amount of lighting time in order to grow plants as quickly as possible without causing them stress.

When you turn on the lighting panel, inspect it

THE UNOFFICIAL AEROGARDEN BIBLE

to make sure that all of the LEDs are working properly. The panel houses many individual LED bulbs and it is important that they all function or your plants will not receive even light.

If all of the lights are working properly, you are ready to get started with your first garden. But before we insert the seed pods, let's make sure the unit is in the right spot.

Ideally, you don't want to have to move your Aerogarden to different places, so it's important to figure out, in advance, where is the best home for it. Keep in mind that the Aerogarden's lights will be on constantly for fifteen hours. Because of this, you will want to keep the Aerogarden in a place where ambient light isn't a problem. Many gardeners put their Aerogarden in the kitchen partly because a little extra light in the kitchen is less disruptive, and because it is an aesthetically pleasing addition to the room.

If you space is limited, you will want to make sure your Aerogarden is in a place that will not disrupt your sleep. The lights are quite bright, so you will want to place it in an area that is separated from the rest of your living space.

If you are using the Family Farm Series, your garden will most likely be placed on the floor. If this is the case, make sure the garden is in a place where it won't be a tripping hazard. And of course, regardless of which Aerogarden you are using, you will need to make sure it is near a power outlet.

WIND AND THE OUTDOORS

When you are deciding where to place you Aerogarden, you might be considering putting it near a window. While this might be a good aesthetic choice, your Aerogarden functions more reliably when it is not near a window. An open window can invite gusts of cold or hot air, which may negatively affect your plants, and it can also let in different molds and insects that might damage your plants.

SAFETY CONCERNS

The Aerogarden is designed to consume and output a very specific amount of power to the lights and the water pump. As a result, it is recommended that you do not use any aftermarket power adapters.

Always make sure children are supervised when using the Aerogarden as the combination of the electrical components and water can be a shock hazard.

Only fill the base of the Aerogarden to the "Fill to Here" line. You do not want to risk damaging the unit by filling it too much. Also, make sure the light panel does not come into contact with water as this can damage the lights.

When cleaning the Aerogarden, make sure the base is unplugged and the water basin is empty.

HOW DO SEED PODS WORK?

One of the great things about the seed pods is that it takes a lot of the guesswork out of planting your seeds. You don't need to worry about how much soil to use, or how deeply to plant the seeds. Each pod contains a growing environment for your plant's root, and this will hold them in place while they grow.

When you order your Aerogarden, you will be given a choice about which seed pods you would like to receive. The Harvest Series can be ordered with the gourmet herb seed kit, the heirloom salad greens kit, the cherry tomato kit, or the cascading petunia seed kit. Regardless of what kit you've chosen, the instructions are the same. Place the seed pods into the holes on the grow deck and place the grow domes over the top of each seed pod. The grow domes are designed to let just the right amount of light into the seed pod to provide the optimal environment for germination.

If you decide that you want to try other seed pod kits, just visit the Aerogarden website to see what is currently available. All of the seed pods work with all of the different Aerogarden models so you can choose whichever kit you'd like. Aerogarden is also constantly coming up with new seed pods so that you can keep experimenting with all kinds of fresh fruits, veggies, herbs, and flowers.

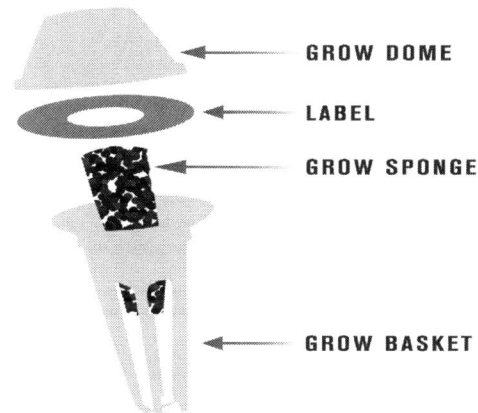

DIY SEED PODS

You might be wondering if you have to use the pods provided by Aerogarden in order to grow with your Aerogarden. The answer is: no. But you will have to fashion your own pods in order for the Aerogarden to work.

If you want to make your own pods, be sure to keep the used pods from your first garden because you will need them to make your own pods. First you will empty out the used pods. Then you will need to add a growing environment to the pod in order to hold the seeds in place as they germinate and develop their root system.

Typically, the best material for this is a soft foam. Your local hardware store probably sells foam that is used for window insulation around an air conditioner. This type of foam is perfect for your Aerogarden pods.

Simply cut the foam into pieces that fit comfortably in the empty Aerogarden pods. You can also go online and order growing sponges from any number of different hydroponic supply companies. These sponges, or your homemade foam, will hold the roots in place as they grow, and they will also soak up just the right amount of water to keep your plants hydrated. Once you've added the sponges and seeds to the pod, you can insert it into the grow deck like you would with a normal seed pod.

If you'd like to use your own seeds or plant cuttings, but you don't want to make your own pods, you can try the Aerogarden Grow Anything Kits. These kits contain grow baskets, the growing sponges, plant food, grow domes,

THE UNOFFICIAL AEROGARDEN BIBLE

and labels to help you keep track of what you are growing.

Unlike the premade seed pods, these are not already assembled, but they are very easy to use. All you have to do it place the grow sponge into the grow basket and push your seeds into the sponge. Then, you will insert the grow basket into the grow deck and place the grow dome over the top of the pod.

As we mentioned, these kits work with most varieties of seeds, but you can also use these kits to transplant cuttings from plants you are already growing. That's right, you can clone your own plants by making cuttings from your existing plants. It might sound like something out of Jurassic Park, but cloning plants is really quite easy. All you need to do is cut a section of the stem of a plant, preferably below one of the leaves. Then, you put the cutting in a shallow glass of water for a few days until it sprouts roots. Once this happens, you can plant the new plant in an Aerogarden seed pod and keep growing it.

It's also a great way to get a head start on outdoor growing season. You can start your plants germinating in the Aerogarden, and then transplant them outdoors as soon as the weather is right. This will help increase the overall size of your plants and will lead to bigger yields when harvest time comes around.

THE GROWING PROCESS

Once you've successfully set up your Aerogarden and inserted the seed pods, it's time to start growing. The first step in the process is called germination. This is when the seeds springs to life because it has come into contact with water. The water activates the seed and its life cycle begins. The Aerogarden allows your seeds to start germinating faster

than seeds grown outdoors in soil, and you should start to notice your first sprouts after about five to seven days, depending on what you are growing.

At first, your little seedlings are quite delicate, and you will want to do everything possible to keep them alive. Don't worry, though, because the Aerogarden is designed to be a stable and even growing environment. In order to keep you plants alive as they grow, all you need to do is make sure the water level is correct and add plant food to the water whenever the food light comes on. This should happen about every two weeks. Otherwise, all you need to do is make sure the Aerogarden stays plugged in so that the lights continue with their cycles.

HARVEST TIME

The time it takes before your plants are ready to be harvested will depend on a few different factors. First, what you are growing will determine how long it takes to come to maturity. Some plants simply take longer than others. Also, if you have a smaller Aerogarden model, you will have to harvest earlier that you would with one of the larger models because your plants will simply outgrow the unit.

For best results, you can use a pair of sharp gardening sheers or scissors to trim the plants or harvest fruits and vegetables. Because the Aerogarden uses a hydroponic system alongside the seed pod system, you won't have to trim the roots of your plants. They will only grow as large as they need to be in order to absorb enough water and nutrition. One of the great things about hydroponic gardening is that the plants are delivered everything they need in order to thrive. This means that they don't have to expend a lot of energy growing extensive root systems to find water or nutrition. That energy can be repurposed to give you faster growing plants and bigger yields.

TROUBLESHOOTING AND WORKAROUNDS

Problem: The lights are flickering

Solution: This is most likely caused by using another electrical appliance in the same outlet as the Aerogarden. It's possible that the appliances are competing for enough electricity and the Aerogarden is not getting enough. To solve this, try moving the other appliance to another outlet.

Problem: Lights have stopped working

Solution: First, make sure that the unit it plugged in and turned on. Next, make sure that the "light" button hasn't been accidentally turned off. You can also try resetting the light cycle if none of these solutions work. Finally, if you find that the lights still don't work, contact Aerogarden about warranty information and part replacement.

Problem: Plants are dying

Solution: Chances are this is a matter of consistency. In order for plants to thrive, they need a very consistent environment. Make sure to keep the water level consistent, and don't change the timing of the light cycle too much. These kinds of inconsistencies can cause the plants to experience stress and die. Also, make sure to feed the plants as often as recommended, but not more often than recommended. Too much plant food can be as harmful as too little food.

Problem: Leaves look limp

Solution: If your leaves are looking limp, the likely problem is a lack of water. Check to make sure that the water levels are correct.

Problem: What if the Aerogarden starts making noise?

Solution: If the water pump is working properly, you should barely hear it. If you notice a buzzing or humming sound, the likely culprit is bad positioning. Try moving the Aerogarden slightly so that it is on a more even level. You can also try removing any loose objects near the Aerogarden.

Problem: The "add food" light has stopped working

Solution: The first thing you should try is resetting the Aerogarden by unplugging it and plugging it back in. Reset the light cycle and see if that solves the problem. If nothing seems to work to resolve the problem, then it may be faulty or broken. In that case, remember it's just a light that conveniently reminds you to add plant food, it doesn't affect the operation of the Aerogarden. Just remember to add plant food to the water every two weeks.

Problem: My lighting timer isn't set correctly. How do I fix it?

Solution: You can change the timing of the light timer at any time by holding down the timer button for three seconds. The lights will flash, and the timer is now reset. Keep in mind when you reset the timer, the lights will stay on for fifteen hours from that point. So, if you want to set the lights to a specific time, make sure to wait until that time to reset the timer.

Problem: Avoiding mildew and other molds

Solution: Make sure your Aerogarden is in a dry space. Ambient moisture can cause mildew and molds, so make sure the area where you are keeping your Aerogarden is dry and not too humid. Some gardeners feel as though they should be spraying their plants or adding extra water to the stems of the plants. With an Aerogarden this is not necessary and can cause the seed pods to retain too much water. This can cause mold growth. Just keep in mind that your Aerogarden is designed to deliver the exact amount of water your plants need in order to thrive. They don't need anything else.

Problem: My herbs don't last very long after being harvested

Solution: Herbs are fragile, and they need to be stored properly. If you want to store fresh herbs, the best way to do it is to keep them on a damp paper towel in a zipperlock bag in the refrigerator. For dried herbs, you want to make sure the herbs are completely dry before storing. Otherwise, they will grow mold and decompose. Place the herbs on dry paper towels and put in a sunny dry place for a few days. Once they are completely dried, they can be crushed or stored whole in airtight containers.

Problem: My seed pod didn't germinate

Solution: Most likely, this is a matter of the pod not getting enough water. First, check to see if the water level is correct. If everything else about the Aerogarden seems to be working properly, chances are the problem is with the pod itself. Because seeds come from nature, they aren't 100% reliable. You may need to try another pod. You can contact Aerogarden directly about getting a replacement pod.

Problem: My Aerogarden is too bright for my space

Solution: Because the Aerogarden uses very powerful LED lights, the unit will be quite bright. When choosing a place for your Aerogarden consider the fact that the lights will be running constantly for fifteen hours. For this reason, it is not recommended to put the Aerogarden in bedrooms. If you only have a small space, you can try tenting the unit with dark fabric, but make sure the fabric does not come into contact with the light panel. Editor's note: Please use common sense, if the fabric comes into contact with the light panel there's a risk of causing a fire or some other damage that could ruin your day.

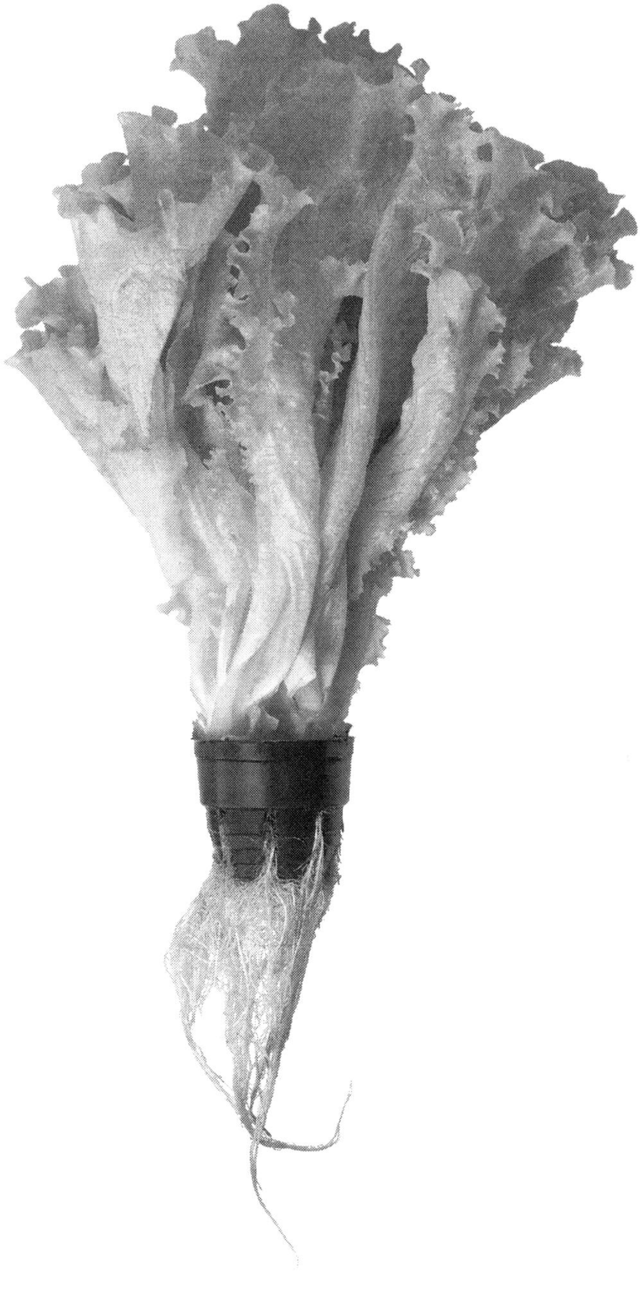

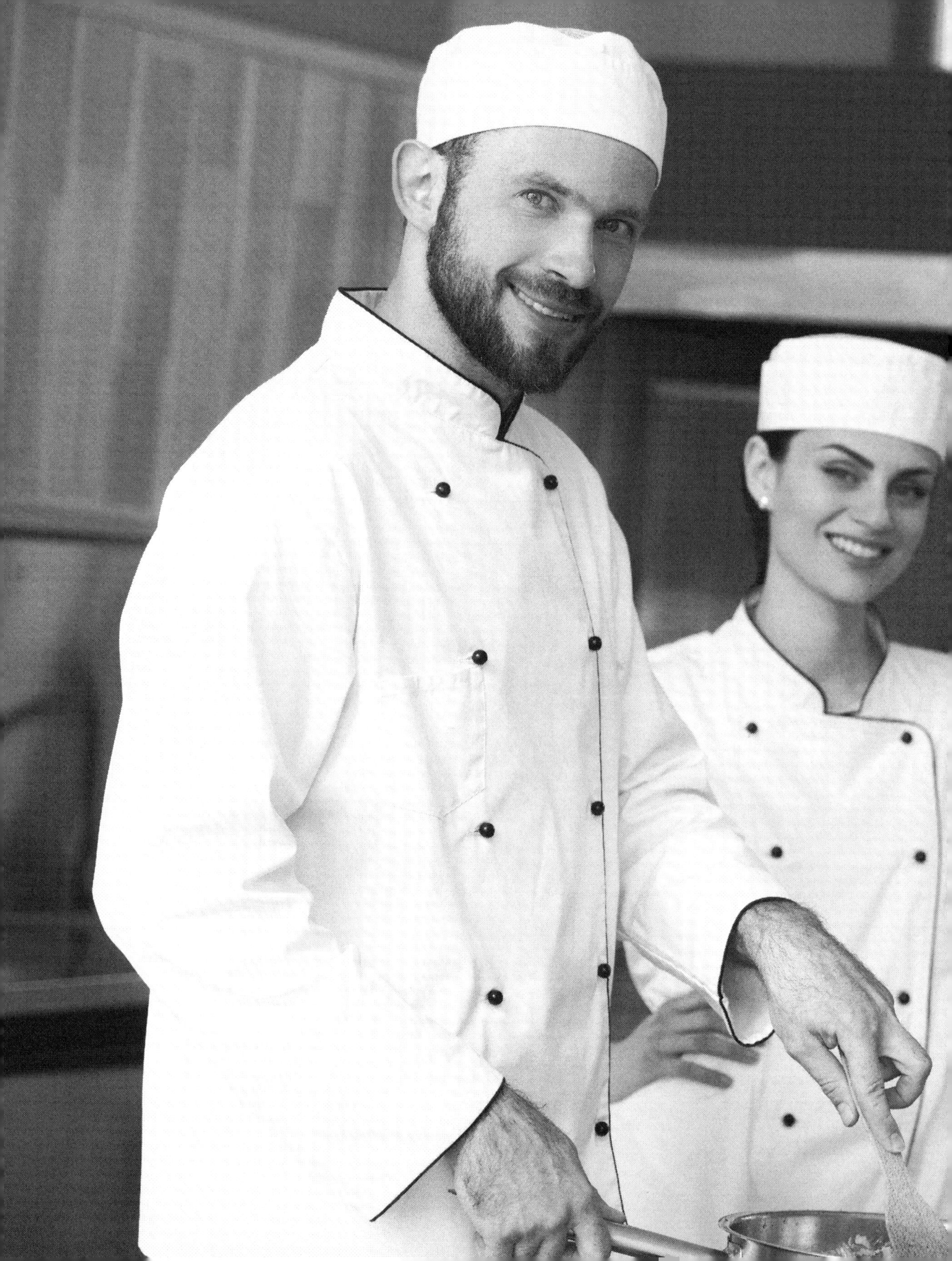

CHAPTER 6
PRO TIPS

HOW TO MAKE SURE THE PH LEVEL OF THE WATER IS CORRECT

The pH level of water is determined by how acidic it is. If the water level is too acidic, your plants won't thrive, however, if the water isn't acidic enough, the plants will not thrive either. The idea pH level for most hydroponic plants is between 5.5 and 6.5. The plant food included with your Aerogarden should help to keep pH levels within that range, but if you want to keep track of your pH level on your own, you can buy a pH meter or paper pH strips that can be dipped in the water and will show the acid level. If you find that, for some reason, your water is too acidic or not acidic enough, you can buy water additives that will raise or lower your pH level.

HOW TO SPACE YOUR PLANTS FOR BEST RESULTS.

This can be a challenge for gardeners of all skill levels. Some plants like lots of elbow room in order to grow, while others like to be packed together more closely. The great things about the Aerogarden is that you don't need to worry about plant spacing at all. The Aerogarden's grow decks are designed to show you exactly where to place you seed pods so that they plants won't be too crowded or too spaced out.

ADDING MORE LIGHT TO YOUR SETUP

Your Aerogarden comes equipped with a high-powered LED light panel, but some gardeners decide they want to take things to the next level. If you are feeling constrained by the amount of light you're getting from the light panel, you can add more by buying some inexpensive LED panels meant for photography. These panels come in square and ring shapes and can be places at the sides of the Aerogarden to add more light to the environment.

If you have a very crowded Aerogarden, this is a great solution because you may be finding that your plants are competing for the light and some of them are not getting enough. This can also be true if you are trying to grow very large plants. You can also buy timers for these additional LED light panels so that they are in sync with the Aerogarden light panel.

When choosing an additional lighting panel, consider models that feature full spectrum light. This is the type of light that is produced by your Aerogarden lighting panel, and it will give your plants a wide range of color temperatures to ensure fast, healthy growth.

HOW TO ADD SUPPORT TO HEAVIER BRANCHES

If you are planning to grow larger plants or plants that have heavy fruit like tomatoes, you may find that your branches are getting a little droopy. In order to fix this, you can get some very thin wooden dowels. These are available at any hardware store. You will also need some string or gardening twine.

All you have to do to add extra support is gently plant the dowel in the growing sponge near the base of the stem. Then cut the twine into small lengths. Tie the heavier branches to the dowels with the twine and this should keep the branches from drooping.

HOW TO TRANSPLANT OR CLONE YOUR PLANTS FROM THE AEROGARDEN

Believe it or not, transplanting and cloning is easier than it sounds. As we mentioned before, the Aerogarden is a great way to get a head start on mother nature. If you want to start your outdoor garden early, you can get everything started in the Aerogarden before the weather is right for outdoor gardening. When it's time to plant outside, you can move your plants from the Aerogarden to your outdoor garden. All you have to do is remove the plant from the Aerogarden, but make sure to keep the grow sponge attached to the roots. This will make the plant easier to move and will prevent the roots from becoming damaged.

Dig a hole in your outdoor garden and place the plant with the grow sponge in the hole. The grow sponge will deteriorate over time as the soil takes hold of the plant's roots.

CLONING A PLANT

In order to clone a plant, you will need to take a cutting from an existing plant. The best place to make the cut is right below where a leaf meets the stem. Once you've made your cuttings, place the bottoms in a shallow glass of water and wait a few days. After a few days the cuttings should begin to sprout little roots. From here, you can either plant the cuttings in an empty Aerogarden seed pod and grow it in your Aerogarden, or you can plant it outdoors in soil. This is a great way to preserve a particularly special or high yielding plant because it will be genetically identical to the plant from which it was cut.

POLLINATING YOUR OWN PLANTS

Pollination is how plants reproduce and it happens in a variety of ways. When plants are grown outdoors, they can be pollinated by the wind or by insects hopping from plant to plant, bringing pollen with them. There are certain plants that are able to self-pollinate, but others need a bit of help. The problem with indoor gardening is that you won't have much wind or insects to do the pollinating. As a result, your plants might need a helping hand. You can do this in a variety of ways, and you should get good results. The first method, if you happen to have a window in the room with your Aerogarden is to let in a cool breeze. This will help circulate the pollen naturally. You can also try giving your plants a gentle shake, which should move some pollen around.

Did you know that plants are male and female just like animals? Well, it's true and in order to create pollination, you need to have a male plant and a female plant. The males are easy to spot because they usually start flowering first. You will notice pollen sacks forming near the leaves of most plants. Female plant, on the other hand, do not produce pollen. In most cases, simply having male and female plants near each other should result in pollination, but you can also help things along by brushing your hand around the male plant and then repeating the motion on the female plant.

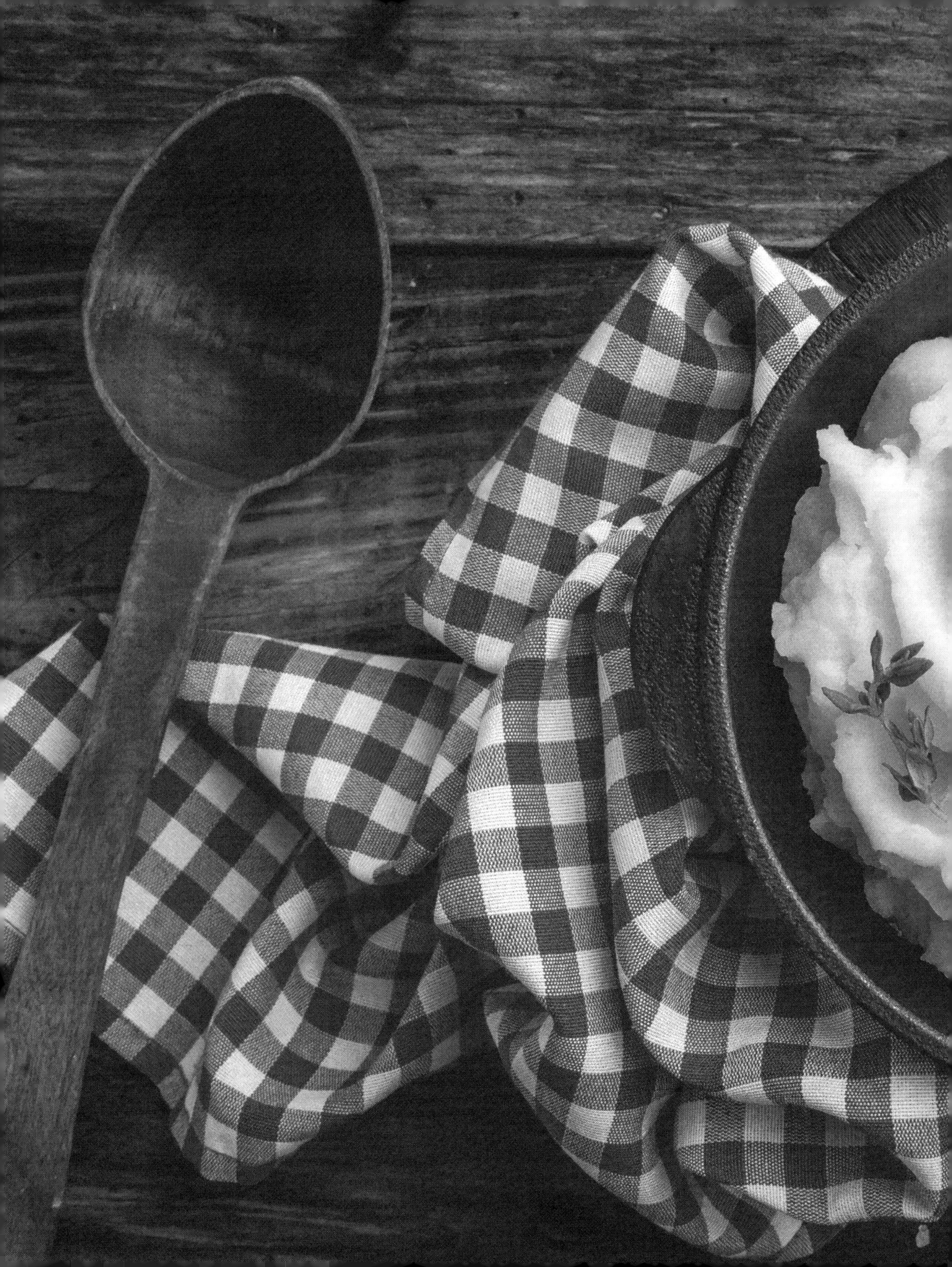

CHAPTER 7
RECIPES

BRUSCHETTA AL POMODORO

Servings: 24 | Prep Time: 31 minutes | Cook Time: 9 minutes | Total Time: 40 minutes

INGREDIENTS

2 pounds ripe tomatoes (approximately 5-6 medium sized tomatoes)

1/2 teaspoon fine sea salt, adjust to taste

1/2 cup white onion, finely chopped

1/2 cup fresh basil, chiffonade

2 cloves garlic, minced

1 baguette

4 - 5 tablespoons extra virgin olive oil

Thick balsamic vinegar, to taste

Maldon salt, to taste

Bruschetta. Who knows how to say it right? We will tell you! It's pronounced as broo-skeh-tuh. Now that's out of the way, let's make it! A light Pinot Grigio with light acidity and crisp texture will go really well with this balanced dish.

DIRECTIONS

1. Preheat the oven to 450° F. Cover a baking sheet with parchment paper.
2. Slice and dice the tomatoes. Try to separate most of the seeds and juice. Put the tomatoes to a mixing bowl. Add in sea salt, onion, garlic, and basil. Mix well and set aside.
3. Slice the baguette on a bias or circles, as per your preference. Toast them in the oven till crispy and golden (about 7 minutes). Arrange on a tray or platter.
4. Remember to put together the bruschetta only when you're ready to serve.
5. Once ready, drain the juices from the tomato mixture and add 2 tablespoons of olive oil. Adjust the sea salt as per your taste. You may also add some more garlic if you want.
6. Spoon each toast with some tomato topping. You can rest your spoon against the side of the bowl to remove excess juices.
7. Drizzle balsamic vinegar, and sprinkle Maldon salt on the bruschetta.
8. Serve immediately so the bruschette don't become soggy.

Nutritional Info: Calories: 40 | Sodium: 56mg | Dietary Fiber: 0.6g | Total Fat: 1.2g | Total Carbs: 3.2g | Protein: 0.7g.

FRESH GREEN SALAD

Servings: 4 | Prep Time: 15 minutes | Total Time: 15 minutes

Healthy and delicious- a fresh green salad will always be in style. The toasted sesame seeds and pine nuts give this salad a crunch that it needs. This perfect starter can be paired well with a zesty white wine like an Albariño or a Sauvignon Blanc.

INGREDIENTS

SALAD:

1/2 cup fresh mint leaves

1-1/2 cups fresh parsley leaves

1/2 cup fresh basil leaves

2 cups fresh baby spinach leaves

4 small radishes, thinly sliced

1 tablespoon sesame seeds, toasted

2 tablespoons pine nuts, toasted

DRESSING:

4 tablespoons extra virgin olive oil

1/2 lemon, juiced

1 tablespoon red wine vinegar or apple cider vinegar

Salt and freshly cracked pepper to taste

DIRECTIONS

1. Take a large bowl and mix the salad ingredients together. Mix in the toasted sesame seeds and pine nuts. Mix gently but thoroughly.
2. Mix together the lemon juice, red wine vinegar, and slowly whisk in the olive oil. Season with salt and pepper.
3. Combine the dressing and the salad mixture or drizzle the dressing over the greens.
4. Serve right away.

Nutritional Info: Calories: 182 | Sodium: 68mg | Dietary Fiber: 2.4g | Total Fat: 18.4g | Total Carbs: 4.7g | Protein: 2.6g.

HOMEMADE MINT ICE CREAM

Servings: 8 | Prep Time: 10 minutes | Cook Time: 10 minutes | Total Time: 20 minutes | Chill Time: 10 hours

INGREDIENTS

2 cups milk

1 cup sugar

2 eggs

1/2 cup light corn syrup

2 cups heavy cream

1/2 teaspoon mint extract

Fresh mint leaves

Perfect as a summer treat, mint ice cream tastes the best at home. Want to go a step further? Blend in the ice cream with some full-cream milk for an amazing milk shake. You may or may not want to add in green food coloring, maybe depending on how close we are to St. Patrick's Day.

DIRECTIONS

1. Make a double boiler and add in the milk. Heat up the milk till some bubbles begin to form.

2. In a mixing bowl, whisk eggs, sugar, and corn syrup. Mix well.

3. Keep the flame on medium. The water should simmer the entire time. Slowly drip in this mixture into the warmed milk, mixing continuously. Keep stirring over the double boiler for about 5 minutes. You will notice that the mixture has thickened to become almost like a custard. If you haven't reached this stage, adjust the heat and keep stirring.

4. Remove the mixture from the heat. Whisk in the heavy cream, and mint extract. Cool this down without putting it in the fridge.

5. Once the mixture (ice cream base) has come down to room temperature, put it in an airtight container and refrigerate for 8 hours, preferably more.

6. Once you have refrigerated the ice cream base for a number of hours, start churning.

7. After churning to the desired consistency, store the ice cream in the freezer.

8. Serve in 2 to 4 hours. You can garnish with the fresh mint leaves.

Nutritional Info: Calories: 298 | Sodium: 56mg | Dietary Fiber: 0g | Total Fat: 13.4g | Total Carbs: 43.7g | Protein: 4g.

INSTANT POT THAI GREEN CURRY

Servings: 4 | Prep Time: 10 minutes | Cook Time: 15 minutes | Total Time: 25 minutes

INGREDIENTS

1 tablespoon canola oil

2 - 4 tablespoons Thai green curry paste

1 can coconut milk

1 large yellow onion, sliced

1 medium zucchini, 1/2 inch pieces (like crudités)

8 ounces cremini mushrooms, quartered

1-1/2 cups Thai eggplant, 1/2 inch cubes

1 teaspoon salt

1 cup snap peas

1 small orange pepper, 2 inch long slices

1 tablespoon brown sugar

1 tablespoon soy sauce

1/2 fresh lime, juiced

1/4 cup fresh cilantro

1/4 cup fresh Thai basil

A fragrant and healthy curry such as this is a keeper. You can whip it up for weeknight dinners or even when your favorite vegetarian visits. You can use tamari or a gluten-free soy sauce, if you prefer. A nice Pinot Gris, Riesling or even a Sauvignon Blanc would work wonderfully with this curry and balance out the spice.

DIRECTIONS

1. Put the Instant Pot to sauté mode. Heat oil and add the green curry paste. Sauté till the curry paste is fragrant. Add in the coconut milk.
2. Add all the vegetables except the snap peas, and season with salt. Mix well.
3. Pressure cook for 1 minute under low pressure.
4. Release the pressure. You can release it manually after letting it rest for 5 minutes.
5. Add the snap peas. Season with brown sugar, soy sauce, pepper, and lime juice. Adjust the seasonings, as required.
6. Sauté till the curry comes to a rolling boil. Cancel the sauté mode. Garnish with the herbs. Cook for 4 to 5 more minutes and serve with jasmine rice.

Nutritional Info: Calories: 313 | Sodium: 1205mg | Dietary Fiber: 10.1g | Total Fat: 21.4g | Total Carbs: 31.5g | Protein: 4.6g.

CHIMICHURRI DE BUENOS AIRES

Servings: 1 - 1 1/2 cups | Prep Time: 15 minutes | Total Time: 15 minutes

INGREDIENTS

1/2 cup parsley, finely chopped

2 tablespoons fresh oregano, finely chopped

4 garlic cloves, crushed

1/2 cup green onions, minced

1 small red chili pepper, de-seeded and finely chopped

2 tablespoons red wine vinegar

1 tablespoon fresh lemon juice

1/2 cup oil

Salt and pepper, to taste

Chimichurri is ubiquitous to Argentina and Uruguay. It is a perfect accompaniment to steak, especially a skirt steak. It can also jazz up your lunch with an addition to salads or sandwiches. You can also use this sauce as a marinade. Malbec is one of the most popular Argentine wines and it pairs famously with a steak and chimichurri sauce.

DIRECTIONS

1. Mix all the ingredients in a bowl. You may substitute the chili pepper with chili flakes if you like it less spicy. You may also add additional herbs like cilantro, basil, thyme, etc.

2. Let it rest in the fridge for 2 hours for the flavors to develop. Refrigerate this sauce and for the best flavor, use it up within 24 to 48 hours.

Nutritional Info: Calories: 283| Sodium: 94mg | Dietary Fiber: 3.3g | Total Fat: 28.7g | Total Carbs: 8.5g | Protein: 2g.

CHERMOULA

Servings: 2 | Prep Time: 10 minutes | Total Time: 10 minutes

INGREDIENTS

1 teaspoon cumin seeds, toasted

1 teaspoon coriander seeds, toasted

1 cup fresh cilantro

1 cup fresh Italian parsley

1 teaspoon fresh ginger

1 teaspoon fresh thyme

2 garlic cloves

1/2 cup olive oil

Zest from 1/2 lemon

2 tablespoons lemon juice

1/4 teaspoon Aleppo chili flakes

1/4 teaspoon salt

Chermoula is a marinade or relish that can be used to flavor different dishes. It is mainly used for seafood but it can also be used for meats, and vegetables. It is a traditional condiment hailing from Algeria, Libya, Tunisia, and Morocco. Light wines like Sancerre or Chenin Blanc works with the flavors of Chermoula.

DIRECTIONS

1. Dry roast the cumin and sesame seeds over medium heat. Keep stirring till the seeds are golden brown and fragrant.
2. Put all the ingredients into a food processor and blend till mixed well. The mixture does not have to be too smooth.
3. If you would like to use this as a marinade, add 1 teaspoon of salt per pound of meat.
4. You can store the Chermoula for up to 4 days in the fridge in an airtight container.

Nutritional Info: Calories: 469| Sodium: 326mg | Dietary Fiber: 1.9g | Total Fat: 51.2g | Total Carbs: 6.8g | Protein: 2g.

CLASSIC AVOCADO TOAST WITH CHERRY TOMATOES

Servings: 6 | Prep Time: 10 minutes | Total Time: 10 minutes

INGREDIENTS

6 slices of French or sourdough bread

1-1/2 - 2 cups of fresh cherry tomatoes, halved

8 fresh basil leaves, chiffonade

2 avocados, mashed

1 tablespoon olive oil

1/2 tablespoon white balsamic vinegar

1 small clove of garlic, minced

1 teaspoon black pepper, freshly ground

2 pinches of salt

No, not eating avocado toast will not help you save on the house you're looking to buy. Actually, you are not even ordering it in, you are making, so that should count for something! Level up on your classic avocado toast with this cherry tomato mix.

DIRECTIONS

1. Put the halved cherry tomatoes and basil chiffonade together in a bowl.
2. Mix the balsamic vinegar, minced garlic, black pepper, a pinch of salt. Whisk in the the olive oil to make a vinaigrette.
3. Marinate the tomatoes with this vinaigrette.
4. Toast the bread slices in the oven/toaster/grill.
5. Arrange the toasted bread as you would serve it.
6. Mash the avocados to the consistency you like. Only mash them once you are ready to serve otherwise they will turn brown.
7. Layer the avocado and the cherry tomatoes with vinaigrette on top of the bread.
8. Sprinkle some salt over the toasts.

Nutritional Info: Calories: 262| Sodium: 265mg | Dietary Fiber: 6g | Total Fat: 16.1g | Total Carbs: 26.5g | Protein: 5.6g.

SHISHITO POPPERS

Servings: 6 | Prep Time: 15 minutes | Cook Time: 5 minutes | Total Time: 20 minutes

INGREDIENTS

1/2 pound fresh shishito peppers

8 ounces cream cheese, softened

4 ounces dry salami, diced

1 teaspoon garlic powder

1/2 teaspoon black pepper, ground

Whenever someone says poppers, does it remind you of a thick breadcrumb coating? Forget those days! This recipe calls for no breading but it amazingly delicious anyway. 5 ingredients and 20 minutes, what are you waiting for?

DIRECTIONS

1. Turn the broiler setting on in your oven.
2. Chop the salami into small pieces. Mix together the salami, softened cream cheese, garlic powder, and ground black pepper.
3. Put the shishito peppers on a parchment paper lined baking tray.
4. Make incisions on the peppers with a paring knife. Make a cut from the stem till the end, make sure only one side is cut and the pepper is not falling apart.
5. Using a teaspoon or a piping bag, fill in the pepper with the mixture. Press the sides so the peppers close.
6. Use cooking oil to spray the stuffed peppers. Broil the peppers for about 5 minutes. The peppers should look blistered and the cheese will become golden brown.
7. Serve immediately.

Nutritional Info: Calories: 196| Sodium: 328mg | Dietary Fiber: 1.8g | Total Fat: 17.4g | Total Carbs: 4.4g | Protein: 6.2g.

PIMIENTOS RELLENOS

Servings: 4 | Prep Time: 15 minutes | Total Time: 55 minutes

INGREDIENTS

4 fresh large bell peppers

1 pound lean (at least 80%) ground beef

2 tablespoons onion, chopped

1 cup rice, cooked

1 teaspoon salt

1 clove garlic, finely chopped

1 can (15 ounces) tomato sauce

3/4 cup mozzarella cheese, shredded

Even though Pimientos Rellenos are traditionally Spanish, different versions of this recipe are found all over Europe and America. It is a classic comfort food and doesn't take a lot of preparation either. It can be paired with a fun, bold wine like a Tempranillo.

DIRECTIONS

1. Preheat the oven to 350°F.
2. Slice off the top of the pepper and remove the seeds and membranes from inside. If the pepper isn't standing on its own, slice off a thin layer from the bottom as well.
3. Wash and clean the peppers. In a 4-quart Dutch oven, heat water (enough to cover the peppers). Boil the water and the peppers. Cook for 2 minutes and drain. Keep aside.
4. Cook the beef and onion over medium heat in a skillet, for 8 to 10 minutes. Once the beef is turning brown, add in rice, garlic, and 1 cup of the tomato sauce. Mix well and cook till it's heated through.
5. Put the peppers in an ungreased baking dish. Make sure they're standing upright. Spoon in the beef mixture into the peppers. Pour the rest of the tomato sauce over the peppers.
6. Cover the peppers well with foil and bake for about 10 minutes. Bake uncovered for 10 more minutes. Then top the peppers with cheese and bake till the peppers are tender and the cheese has melted.
7. Sprinkle some freshly chopped parsley or oregano before serving.

Nutritional Info: Calories: 452| Sodium: 801mg | Dietary Fiber: 2.7g | Total Fat: 8.7g | Total Carbs: 50.3g | Protein: 41.2g.

BASIL PESTO

Servings: 1 | Prep Time: 15 minutes

INGREDIENTS

2 cups fresh basil leaves, packed (can substitute half the basil leaves with baby spinach)

1/2 cup Romano or Parmesan-Reggiano cheese, grated

1/2 cup extra virgin olive oil

1/3 cup pine nuts

3 garlic cloves, minced

1/4 teaspoon salt, more to taste

1/8 teaspoon black pepper, freshly ground

This is a classic pesto recipe. Pesto can also be made with different kinds of greens and different nuts but the original recipe always includes basil and pine nuts. Pesto can be used as a pasta sauce, sandwich spread, or even as a dip. You can also mix in a spoonful or two of mayonnaise to make a creamy dip for something like chicken fingers.

DIRECTIONS

1. Blend the basil and pine nuts in a blender. Make sure to pulse it.
2. Mix in the garlic, cheese and pulse some more.
3. While blending, stream in the olive oil slowly and keep the blender running. The olive oil is slowly added and mixed so as to emulsify the pesto. Scrape down the sides with a spatula and mix everything in.
4. Add in salt, pepper, and adjust the seasonings to taste.
5. Store in an airtight container, and put some plastic wrap over the pesto so it doesn't come in contact with any air. As pesto oxidizes when it comes in contact with air, it is best to keep it covered so it doesn't become dark in colour.

Nutritional Info: Calories: 1249| Sodium: 756mg | Dietary Fiber: 2.7g | Total Fat: 136g | Total Carbs: 10.9g | Protein: 12.8g.

CLASSIC MEATBALLS

Servings: 4 | Prep Time: 20 minutes | Total Time: 30 minutes

INGREDIENTS

8 ounces ground beef chuck

8 ounces ground pork

1-1/2 cups panko

1 large egg, lightly beaten

1 garlic clove, minced

1 teaspoon fresh rosemary, finely chopped

1 tablespoon lemon zest

1 tablespoon fresh lemon juice

Coarse salt and ground pepper, to taste

1 tablespoon olive oil

4 cups homemade tomato sauce

Meatballs are easy to make but they elevate any meal they are a part of! Use these as a filling for your subs, as a side dish to rice or even on some spaghetti.

DIRECTIONS

1. Combine together beef, pork, panko, egg, garlic, chopped rosemary, lemon zest, lemon juice, salt and pepper, to taste. Mix but don't over mix.

2. Use the 1/4 cup as a measurement for each meatball. You may be able to form 12 meatballs. Put these meatballs on a sheet pan lined with parchment paper.

3. Heat up oil in a large skillet on a medium-high flame. Cook the meatballs till they are brown in color. It should take about 10 to 12 minutes.

4. Pour in the tomato sauce and cook over medium-high to medium heat. Cook till the meatballs are done, should take about 8 minutes.

5. Garnish with more rosemary, if you like.

Nutritional Info: Calories: 641| Sodium: 745mg | Dietary Fiber: 5.8g | Total Fat: 32.3g | Total Carbs: 43.3g | Protein: 44.1g.

SPAGHETTI WITH FRESH TOMATO AND BASIL

Servings: 3–4 | Prep Time: 5 minutes | Cook Time: 20 minutes | Total Time: 25 minutes

INGREDIENTS

8–10 ounces thin spaghetti

1/4 cup olive or avocado oil

2 pints fresh cherry tomatoes, cut in half

3–4 medium garlic cloves, thinly sliced

Salt and pepper, to taste

1/4 – 1/2 cup fresh basil, chiffonade

Grated parmesan, optional

Under 10 ingredients and under 30 minutes of cooking time! This dish is perfect for those weeknights when you are exhausted and want something comforting to eat. A crisp white wine like a Pinot Grigio or even a light Sicilian red wine is what you should reach for, to go with this pasta.

DIRECTIONS

1. Bring a large pot of water to boil. Make sure to salt it so it 'tastes like the sea'.
2. Cook the spaghetti as per packet instructions. But cook it a little less as it will cook more in the pan. Drain but save 1 cup of pasta water.
3. While the spaghetti is cooking, begin making the sauce. In a large sauté pan, heat oil over medium heat.
4. Add garlic to the oil and stir fry for a bit. Then add the tomatoes and cook till the tomatoes soften. Press the tomatoes a bit to release the juices. Cook over medium heat so as to not burn the garlic.
5. Bring the pan to medium heat and add the pasta along with the basil. Mix in well and add the reserved pasta water to emulsify the sauce. Taste and adjust seasoning. If using, top with freshly grated Parmesan.

Nutritional Info: Calories: 268| Sodium: 349mg | Dietary Fiber: 5.5g | Total Fat: 16.8g | Total Carbs: 26.8g | Protein: 6.4g.

HONEYED CARROTS

Servings: 4 | Prep Time: 5 minutes | Cook Time: 30 minutes | Total Time: 35 minutes

A perfect side dish for Thanksgiving or Christmas! Carrots roasted with seasoned honey might become your next favorite thing. To make the taste even richer, you may add a dollop of butter.

INGREDIENTS

1 pound fresh small carrots, peeled and trimmed

2 tablespoons olive oil

2 tablespoons honey

Salt and pepper, to taste

Cooking spray, as needed

Fresh parsley, chopped

DIRECTIONS

1. Preheat the oven to 400°F. Line a baking sheet with foil and cover with cooking spray.
2. Put the carrots in a single layer on the baking sheet.
3. In a bowl, mix together the honey, olive oil, salt and pepper. Pour this mixture over the carrots and mix well to coat.
4. Bake the carrots for 25 to 35 minutes, until the carrots are softened and browned.
5. Serve immediately, garnish with parsley.

Nutritional Info: Calories: 101| Sodium: 7mg | Dietary Fiber: 0.5g | Total Fat: 7.1g | Total Carbs: 10.2g | Protein: 0.3g.

ARUGULA SALAD WITH CITRUS

Servings: 4 | Prep Time: 10 minutes | Total Time: 10 minutes

INGREDIENTS

2 small tangerines, peeled and sliced

1 medium blood orange, peeled and sliced

3 cups packed fresh baby arugula

2 tablespoons lime juice

2 tablespoons extra-virgin olive oil

1 tablespoon fresh tarragon, chopped

2 teaspoons fresh jalapeño, finely chopped

1/4 teaspoon salt

1 avocado, chopped

The brightness of citrus, pepperiness of arugula, creaminess of avocado, and the slight kick of jalapeños, makes this the perfect salad course. Choose a fuller white wine like an oak-aged Chardonnay to go with this salad.

DIRECTIONS

1. Combine all the ingredients, other than the arugula and mix well.
2. Slowly toss the mixture with the arugula, and serve.

Nutritional Info: Calories: 1001| Sodium: 715mg | Dietary Fiber:34.5g | Total Fat: 71.5g | Total Carbs: 87.9g | Protein: 16.9g.

CAESAR SALAD WITH GRILLED ROMAINE

Servings: 4 | Prep Time: 20 minutes | Total Time: 20 minutes

This is a new style of serving a Caesar salad. We have all had the creamy salad dressing with the same old romaine. This recipe shows you how to grill different components of the salad and serve it together.

INGREDIENTS

- 3 tablespoons mayonnaise
- 2 tablespoons Worcestershire sauce
- 2 lemons, halved
- 1 tablespoon fresh lemon juice
- 1 tablespoon Dijon mustard
- 1 teaspoon red wine vinegar
- 2 cloves garlic, minced
- 3/4 cup extra-virgin olive oil, plus more for grilling
- 1/4 cup Parmesan, freshly grated
- Kosher salt and freshly ground black pepper, to taste
- 2 hearts fresh romaine lettuce, cut in half lengthwise
- Three 3/4-inch slices rustic bread, like a baguette
- 1 tablespoon sugar

DIRECTIONS

1. Heat the grill to medium-high heat.
2. Whisk together the mayonnaise, Worcestershire sauce, lemon juice, mustard, vinegar and garlic. Slowly stream in the olive oil and whisk it in. Add the Parmesan cheese and combine well. Adjust the seasoning with salt, and pepper.
3. Coat the romaine hearts with olive oil, salt, and pepper. Grill the romaine with the cut-side down. Cook for 2 to 3 minutes, or till you can see the grill marks.
4. Brush the bread slices with olive oil and grill both sides. Cut into croutons.
5. Top the cut-side of the lemons with sugar and grill them till charred.
6. Serve together, the romaine hearts, croutons, grilled lemons, with the salad dressing from step 2.

Nutritional Info: Calories: 433| Sodium: 859mg | Dietary Fiber:1g | Total Fat: 43.3g | Total Carbs: 11g | Protein: 4g.

CILANTRO AND TOMATO CHICKEN

Servings: 8 | Total Time: 40 minutes

INGREDIENTS

2 large fresh plum tomatoes, coarsely grated

2 garlic cloves, minced

1/2 cup olive oil

1/2 cup fresh cilantro, chopped

4 pounds skinless, boneless chicken breasts, cut into 2-inch pieces

Vegetable oil, for brushing

Salt and freshly ground pepper, to taste

Another recipe with less than 10 ingredients, perfect for a weeknight, or even those weekends when you're too tired to cook. Just marinate it all and let it cook. You can marinate it overnight for a quick dinner the next day. This dish is brilliant by itself but can also be eaten with a heaping portion of hot rice or egg noodles.

DIRECTIONS

1. Mix together the chicken with tomatoes, garlic, olive oil, and cilantro. Leave to marinate overnight in the fridge.
2. Heat up the grill. Thread the chicken into skewers. Brush with oil, season with salt, and pepper.
3. Grill over medium heat, till cooked and slightly charred.

Nutritional Info: Calories: 566| Sodium: 1074mg | Dietary Fiber: 0.6g | Total Fat: 31.2g | Total Carbs: 2.6g | Protein: 66.2g.

SALSA FRESCA

Servings: 6 – 8 | Prep Time: 10 minutes | Total Time: 10 minutes | Chill Time: 2 hours

INGREDIENTS

3 tablespoons onion, finely chopped

2 small cloves garlic, minced

3 large ripe tomatoes, peeled, seeds removed, chopped

2 chili peppers, chopped (jalapeño or serrano)

2 to 3 tablespoons fresh cilantro, chopped

1-1/2 tablespoons lime juice, plus more to taste

Salt, to taste

Freshly ground black pepper, to taste

10 minutes of preparation and delicious to boot! This salsa recipe will render that jarred stuff useless. Don't want to take our word? Try this recipe instead.

DIRECTIONS

1. Strain the chopped onion and garlic, by putting 2 cups of boiling water run through them. Cool and drain.
2. Mix the onion and garlic with tomatoes, peppers, cilantro, lime juice, salt, and pepper. Adjust the seasoning.
3. Refrigerate for at least 2 hours to deepen the flavors.
4. This fresh salsa will keep for up to 3 days in the refrigerator.
5. Serve as a sauce, dip, spread, or anything you fancy.

Nutritional Info: Calories: 20| Sodium: 24mg | Dietary Fiber: 1.1g | Total Fat: 0.2g | Total Carbs: 4.7g | Protein: 0.9g.

CREAMY MASHED POTATOES

Servings: 10-12 | Prep Time: 20 minutes | Cook Time: 20 minutes | Total Time: 40 minutes

INGREDIENTS

5-1/2 pounds fresh potatoes, peeled and cubed

3 teaspoons salt, divided

1 cup sour cream

1/2 cup milk

1/4 cup butter, cubed

1/4 cup fresh chives, minced

1 teaspoon pepper

Quick and easy, great for an everyday meal but also special enough to serve to guests. Sour cream gives these mashed potatoes a much-needed tang. Enjoy as a side with any meal.

DIRECTIONS

1. Cook potatoes with 1 teaspoon of salt, until they are cooked. Drain them.
2. Mash the drained potatoes, and add in the sour cream, milk, and butter. Once combined, add in the chives (save some for garnish), salt and pepper. Mix well.
3. Garnish with some chopped chives.

Nutritional Info: Calories: 230| Sodium: 694mg | Dietary Fiber: 5g | Total Fat: 9g | Total Carbs: 34g | Protein: 4.6g.

ASIAN-STYLE SALAD

Servings: 4 | Prep Time:15 minutes | Total Time: 15 minutes

INGREDIENTS

4 tablespoons sweet chili dipping sauce

1 lime, zested

2 tablespoon lime juice

1 teaspoon fish sauce

1 fresh Little Gem lettuce , separated into leaves

2 fresh carrots, thin batons

10 fresh radishes, sliced

4 spring onions, diagonally cut

A handful cilantro, roughly chopped

This Asian-Style salad is bright, crunchy, fresh and has a kick of fish sauce. Make it as a side dish for your next Asian inspired dinner. It will also brighten up any dinner spread so use it as you please.

DIRECTIONS

1. Make the dressing by mixing the chili sauce, lime zest, lime juice, and fish sauce.
2. Mix everything (except lettuce) together with the dressing. Add to the lettuce once you are ready to serve.

Nutritional Info: Calories: 61| Sodium: 344mg | Dietary Fiber: 2g | Total Fat: 0.2g | Total Carbs: 12.8g | Protein: 1.2g.

ZUCCHINI SOUP WITH BASIL

Servings: 2-3 | Prep Time: 5 minutes | Cook Time: 20 minutes | Total Time: 25 minutes

INGREDIENTS

1 medium fresh onion, diced

2 tablespoons olive oil

4 garlic cloves

1-1/2 pounds fresh sliced zucchini

2 cups water or vegetable stock

3/4 teaspoon salt, more to taste

Black pepper, cracked, to taste

1/2 teaspoon white vinegar

1 cup fresh basil leaves, packed, plus more for garnish

GARNISH:

Plain yogurt or sour cream (optional)

Healthy, and delicious! Perfect for a light lunch. This soup feels like a hug on a rainy evening. Yes, it's that good. You can even substitute the basil for mint or cilantro, if you want.

DIRECTIONS

1. Heat oil over medium heat, add onion and sauté till they are tender (about 2 to 3 minutes).
2. Add chopped garlic, and continue stirring for 3 to 4 minutes on a medium-low flame.
3. Wait for the garlic to be golden and fragrant. Add the sliced zucchini, water or vegetable stock, salt, and pepper.
4. Bring to a simmer over high heat, and then turn the heat down to medium low, cover and simmer for 15 minutes. Give it a stir in about 8 minutes.
5. Once the zucchini is tender and translucent, blend in batched with the basil.
6. Blend carefully so you do not burn yourself. Start on a low speed and increase gradually. The soup should be very smooth and the blender should be covered with a kitchen towel to avoid splatters or blender explosion.
7. Return the blended soup to the pot. Stir in vinegar, adjust the seasoning.
8. While serving, garnish with basil chiffonade, and yogurt or sour cream.

Nutritional Info: Calories: 186| Sodium: 677mg | Dietary Fiber: 3.6g | Total Fat: 10.8g | Total Carbs: 18.7g | Protein: 6.2g.

TURKEY STUFFING

Servings: 8 – 10 | Total Time: 50 minutes:

No need to scour the internet for the perfect herbaceous turkey stuffing recipe, you have got one right here! The herbs will brighten up the stuffing and in turn the turkey. It can be made under an hour, which is a big plus!

INGREDIENTS

- 3 tablespoons olive oil, plus more for pan
- 1 loaf country bread, cut into 1/2-inch pieces
- 2 medium onions, chopped
- Kosher salt and freshly ground black pepper
- 4 stalks celery, chopped
- 3 cups chicken stock
- 1 cup fresh flat-leaf parsley, chopped
- 2 teaspoons fresh thyme leaves
- 2 large eggs, beaten

DIRECTIONS

1. Preheat the oven to 375°F. Brush oil into a 2-quart shallow casserole dish or a 3-quart if not stuffing the turkey.
2. Toast the bread in a rimmed baking sheet, stir once and toast till golden brown.
3. Heat oil in a large skillet over medium heat. Add in onions, salt and pepper. Cook till golden brown, and then add celery. Stir and cook till celery is tender. Add the stock and bring to a boil. Add in the thyme, and parsley.
4. In a bowl, mix together the bread, vegetables, stock, and eggs. Mix well and stuff into the turkey or add to the prepared baking dish.
5. Cover the dish with foil and bake for 10 minutes, then bake uncovered till golden brown.

Nutritional Info: Calories: 749| Sodium: 2844mg | Dietary Fiber: 9.5g | Total Fat: 55.6g | Total Carbs: 46.7g | Protein: 22.5g.

FRITTATA WITH TOMATOES

Servings: 4 | Prep Time: 30 minutes

INGREDIENTS

FRITTATA:

8 extra large eggs

1/4 cup finely grated Reggiano Parmesan

2 tablespoons fresh thyme leaves

1 tablespoon fresh oregano, finely chopped

1/2 teaspoon sea salt

Black pepper, freshly ground, to taste

3 tablespoons extra virgin olive oil

TOMATOES:

3 tablespoons extra virgin olive oil

4 large garlic cloves, finely chopped

1/4 cup Italian parsley, finely chopped

1 1/2 pounds medium ripe tomatoes, seeded and cut in 1? pieces

1/4 teaspoon sea salt

Black pepper, freshly ground, to taste

This classic Italian dish can be eaten at any time of the day. Just because it has eggs, don't just consider it as breakfast food! Play around with the sides or toppings and you can have a new recipe every time.

DIRECTIONS

1. Whisk together the eggs, Parmesan, thyme, oregano, salt and pepper. Keep aside.
2. Heat up oil in a large, heavy-bottomed skillet. Add garlic, parsley, and sauté till the parsley starts to wilt. Add the tomatoes and cook till they soften but not falling apart. Add salt, and pepper, and set aside to cool.
3. In a large, non-stick, frying pan, add the olive oil, over medium-heat. Spread the oil evenly. Add the egg mixture. With a spatula, loosen the edges and tilt the pan so the uncooked egg mixtures fills in any bare spots and the egg is cooked evenly.
4. As the eggs begin to set, spoon the tomatoes on top, reduce heat to medium and continue cooking until the frittata is almost set and the bottom is golden brown. Once the bottom is golden brown, flip the frittata with the help of a plate and keep cooking till the other side is set.
5. Transfer to a large plate and serve with greens and a warm potato salad.

Nutritional Info: Calories: 1499| Sodium: 1002mg | Dietary Fiber: 11.1g | Total Fat: 128.2g | Total Carbs: 41.5g | Protein: 60.9g.

HUMMUS WITH JALAPEÑOS

Servings: 8 | Prep Time: 10 minutes | Total Time: 10 minutes

INGREDIENTS

1 cup garbanzo beans, cooked

1/3 cup fresh jalapeños, sliced

3 tablespoons tahini

3 cloves garlic, minced

2 tablespoons lemon juice

1/2 teaspoon ground cumin

1/2 teaspoon curry powder

Crushed red pepper, to taste

A hummus with the kick of jalapeños. This can be used as a dip, spread or anything you like. Adjust the amount of jalapeños as per your spice tolerance.

DIRECTIONS

1. In a food processor, mix together the garbanzo beans, jalapeños, tahini, garlic, and lemon juice. Add the cumin powder, curry powder, and crushed red pepper. Adjust seasoning and blend till smooth.

Nutritional Info: Calories: 132| Sodium: 25mg | Dietary Fiber: 5.2g | Total Fat: 4.7g | Total Carbs: 17.6g | Protein: 6.1g.

ASIAN-STYLE GRILLED CHICKEN WRAPS

Servings: 4 | Prep Time: 20 minutes | Cook Time: 17 minutes | Total Time: 37 minutes

INGREDIENTS

4 (8-ounce) boneless, skinless chicken breasts

Extra-virgin olive oil, as needed

Kosher salt and freshly ground black pepper, to taste

1/2 cup mango-peach jam

2 tablespoons soy sauce

1 teaspoon fresh lime juice

1 teaspoon ginger, peeled and grated

1/2 small jalapeño, seeded, ribs removed, minced

12 ounces fresh Boston or Bibb lettuce, leaves separated

3 green onions, sliced diagonally

DIRECTIONS

1. Heat up the grill to medium-high heat.
2. Mix the chicken with olive oil, and season with salt, and pepper. Grill the chicken until golden brown. Cook both sides till golden brown.
3. Mix mango-peach jam, soy sauce, lime juice, ginger, and jalapeño in a saucepan. Simmer the mixture till it becomes a glaze and the flavors mix in well together.
4. Brush the chicken with the glaze in the last minute of cooking. Remove the chicken from the grill and brush with the glaze again, and slice.
5. Shred with a fork and put the chicken in lettuce cups. Top with green onions. Serve with smoky corn salsa.

Nutritional Info: Calories: 492| Sodium: 692mg | Dietary Fiber: 1.4g | Total Fat: 20.6g | Total Carbs: 6.5g | Protein: 67g.

RED WINE VINAIGRETTE

Servings: 10 | Prep Time: 15 minutes | Total Time: 15 minutes

This is a typical Italian-style vinaigrette that brightens up any salad. Easy to make and tastes great as an addition to vegetable salads, any mixed greens or even in a pasta salad.

INGREDIENTS

4 medium cloves garlic, minced

1/4 cup extra-virgin olive oil

1/4 cup red wine vinegar

2 tablespoons freshly squeezed lemon juice

2 tablespoons fresh oregano, chopped

1 tablespoon Dijon mustard

1-1/2 tsp kosher salt

1 teaspoon sugar

1/4 teaspoon black pepper, freshly ground

DIRECTIONS

1. Make the vinaigrette by mixing all the ingredients well with a whisk or immersion blender.
2. Toss with greens.
3. This vinaigrette can be stored in an air-tight container for two days in the refrigerator. Make sure to remove the vinaigrette from the fridge 30 minutes and shake vigorously before using.

Nutritional Info: Calories: 56| Sodium: 252mg | Dietary Fiber: 0.5g | Total Fat: 5.2g | Total Carbs: 2.4g | Protein: 0.4g.

MINT MOJITO

Servings: 1 | Prep Time: 10 minutes

INGREDIENTS

5 mint leaves, more for garnish

2 ounces white rum

1 ounce fresh lime juice

1/2 ounce simple syrup

Ice

Club soda or sparkling water

Lime slices, for garnish

Can't go to Caribbean? We bring the Caribbean to you! Make a big batch of this refreshing drink and you're good to go for any balmy evening.

DIRECTIONS

1. Muddle the mint. Add rum, lime juice, simple syrup, some ice and shake everything together.
2. Strain into a glass filled with ice. Add a splash of club soda and garnish with lime, and mint.

Nutritional Info: Calories: 254| Sodium: 123mg | Dietary Fiber: 9.8g | Total Fat: 1g | Total Carbs: 30.9g | Protein: 4.3g.

ZOODLES WITH TOMATOES

Servings: 4 | Prep Time : 5 minutes | Cook Time: 5 minutes | Total Time: 10 minutes

Zucchini noodles with tomatoes, basil, and parmesan make for an amazing summer deal. Any light white wine will go well with this dish.

INGREDIENTS

2 medium zucchini, spiralized

2 tablespoons extra virgin olive oil

1 clove garlic, minced

1 cup grape or cherry tomatoes, sliced

1/2 teaspoon red pepper flakes, crushed

Cracked black pepper and kosher salt to taste

2 tablespoons Parmesan, grated

2 tablespoons or more fresh basil torn

DIRECTIONS

1. Spiralize the zucchini.
2. Heat up olive oil in a skillet over medium heat. Sauté the zucchini for 3 minutes. Add the garlic and cook for 1 minute. Add the sliced cherry tomatoes till they're heated through. Add in the crushed red pepper flakes, salt, and pepper. Combine everything together.
3. Take away from heat and add in fresh basil, and freshly grated Parmesan. Mix well together.
4. You can serve this as a side to salmon or as a light dinner by itself.

Nutritional Info: Calories: 133| Sodium: 170mg | Dietary Fiber: 1.3g | Total Fat: 10.1g | Total Carbs: 6.9g | Protein: 5.3g.

KALE CAESAR SALAD

Servings: 6 – 8 | Prep Time: 25 minutes | Total Time: 25 minutes

INGREDIENTS

KALE CAESAR SALAD INGREDIENTS:

4 cups fresh kale, chopped

4 cups fresh Romaine lettuce, chopped

2 cups croutons

3/4 cup Parmesan cheese, grated

1 batch Lime Caesar Dressing, below

OPTIONAL:

1 cup cherry or grape tomatoes, halved

LIME CAESAR DRESSING INGREDIENTS:

1/2 cup plain Greek yogurt

1/2 cup Parmesan cheese, grated

3–4 tablespoons fresh lime juice

1 tablespoon extra-virgin olive oil

1–2 teaspoons anchovy paste, to taste

2 teaspoons Worcestershire sauce

1 clove garlic, pressed or finely minced

1 teaspoon Dijon mustard

1/4 teaspoon sea salt

A pinch of black pepper

3–4 tablespoons milk

This is a super healthy salad with tons of fresh ingredients. The lime Caesar dressing can be stored in an air-tight container for up to 3 days.

DIRECTIONS

1. Make croutons by drizzling olive oil, or butter, salt, and Italian seasoning on bread and toasting. Crumble or chop the toasted bread.
2. Toss all the croutons and greens together.
3. Whisk in all the ingredients for the lime Caesar dressing except the milk. Whisk in the milk slowly and let it reach the desired consistency.
4. Toss with the greens and serve immediately, or refrigerate.

Nutritional Info: Calories: 142| Sodium: 276mg | Dietary Fiber: 1.4g | Total Fat: 4.6g | Total Carbs: 17g | Protein: 11.7g.

RISOTTO WITH FRESH HERBS

Servings: 4 | Prep Time: 45 minutes

INGREDIENTS

7 cups chicken stock or vegetable stock

4 garlic cloves, minced, separated

2 cups fresh herbs, such as parsley, tarragon, chives, chervil, dill, basil, chives, finely chopped

4 cups arugula

2 tablespoons extra virgin olive oil

2/3 cup onion or leek, finely chopped

Salt, preferably kosher salt, to taste

1-1/2 cups arborio or carnaroli rice

1/2 cup dry white wine, such as Pinot Grigio or Sauvignon Blanc

Freshly ground pepper, to taste

1 teaspoon lemon zest

1 tablespoon lemon juice, freshly squeezed

1/2 cup Parmesan, freshly grated

Risottos with greens or bright herbs can be paired with citrus-based white wines, such as Pinot Grigio or Viognier. You can cook the risotto in steps. Cook halfway and then finish cooking once you are ready to serve.

DIRECTIONS

1. Bring the stock to a simmer.
2. Mix the herbs with 1 clove of garlic in a bowl.
3. Heat oil over medium heat in a skillet. Add the leeks or onions, salt, and cook till the onions/leeks are tender.
4. Mix in the rice and the remaining garlic. Stir till the grains begin to crackle. Add the wine and cook till it is absorbed completely.
5. Slowly add in the stock, about 1/2 cup at a time. The stock should never be too much, it should just cover the rice. The stock should also just simmer and not boil. Once the rice is almost tender, adjust the seasoning. The cook time on this should be about 20 to 25 minutes.
6. Add another half cup of stock. Mix in the herbs, pepper, lemon zest, lemon juice, and Parmesan. Remove from heat. The mixture should be creamy. Serve immediately.

Nutritional Info: Calories: 429| Sodium: 737mg | Dietary Fiber: 7.5g | Total Fat: 17.8g | Total Carbs: 48.6g | Protein: 20.5g.

RANCH DRESSING

Servings: 1 cup | Prep Time: 12 minutes

Who doesn't love ranch dressing? You can use it as a dip or as a salad dressing. Goes amazingly well with fried chicken fingers.

INGREDIENTS

1/2 cup low fat mayonnaise

1/2 cup buttermilk or sour milk

2 tablespoons fresh chives, finely chopped

1 tablespoon fresh flat leaf parsley, chopped

1 tablespoon dill, chopped

1 tablespoon onion, chopped

1/2 teaspoon dry mustard

1/4 teaspoon each salt and pepper

1 clove garlic, minced

DIRECTIONS

1. To make the sour milk, combine 1/2 cup of milk and 1-1/2 teaspoon fresh lemon juice. Let it sit for 15 minutes.
2. Blend all the ingrdients together to make a smooth dressing. Store in the refrigerator.

Nutritional Info: Calories: 30| Sodium: 100mg | Dietary Fiber: 0g | Total Fat: 2.5g | Total Carbs: 1.0g | Protein: 0.4g.

Printed in Great Britain
by Amazon